How to Become a Great Life Coach

Positively Influence People with Your Life Coaching Skills and Leadership

~

A Life Coaching Guide: Steps on How to Start Your Life Coaching Business Career

Jan Morgan

Copyright © 2015 Jan Morgan

All rights reserved.

ISBN: 151464990X
ISBN-13: 978-1514649909

TABLE OF CONTENTS

	Introduction	04
CH 1	What is Life Coaching	08
CH 2	The Purpose of Life Coaching	11
CH 3	Areas in Your Life a Life Coach Can Assist	13
CH 4	Your Identity and Reason	17
CH 5	The Qualities of a Great Life Coach	20
CH 6	Life Coach Specialization	24
CH 7	Starting Your Life Coach Career	27
	Conclusion	30

Introduction

I want to thank you and congratulate you for purchasing the book

"How to Become a Great Life Coach. Help and Positively Influence People with Your Powerful Life Coaching and Leadership Skills".

This book contains all the basic information you need to know about becoming a great life coach. Not just any life coach, but a life coach who has influence and strong leadership skills.

If you're reading this book, you probably think becoming a life coach is a dream job. Not only will you be able to help people, but the idea that you can do it from the comforts of your home just makes it better. But of course, you can't just take a training course and quickly call yourself a life coach. You need to work on becoming the best life coach you can be.

Just like with anything else worth having in this world, becoming a great life coach isn't going to be an easy task. It will require you to dig deep within yourself to know if you're cut out for this profession. Since you'll be impacting peoples' lives, you need to fully understand the goal of coaching – helping other people live better lives.

In this book you'll learn the difference between a therapist and a coach. You'll also learn how to identify your purpose and reason that will drive you to become the best life coach you can possibly be. There's also information on how to choose your specialization and get started on your coaching career. With the right information and strong motivation, you'll be able to help change peoples' lives in no time.

Thanks again for downloading this book, I hope you enjoy it!

Copyright © 2015 – Jan Morgan

All rights reserved. No part of this book may be reproduced in any form without permission in writing from the author. Reviewers may quote brief passages in reviews.

Disclaimer

No part of this publication may be reproduced or transmitted in any form or by any means, mechanical or electronic, including photocopying or recording, or by any information storage and retrieval system, or transmitted by email without permission in writing from the publisher.

While all attempts and efforts have been made to verify the information held within this publication, neither the author nor the publisher assumes any responsibility for errors, omissions, or opposing interpretations of the content herein.

This book is for entertainment purposes only. The views expressed are those of the author alone, and should not be taken as expert instruction or commands. The reader of this book is responsible for his or her own actions when it comes to reading the book.

Adherence to all applicable laws and regulations, including international, federal, state, and local governing professional licensing, business practices, advertising, and all other aspects of doing business in the US, Canada, or any other jurisdiction is the sole responsibility of the purchaser or reader.

Neither the author nor the publisher assumes any responsibility or liability whatsoever on the behalf of the purchaser or reader of these materials.

Any received slight of any individual or organization is purely unintentional.

CHAPTER 1

What is Life Coaching?

As a life coach, one of the first things that you need to do is explain to people what exactly you do. Since life coaching isn't really one of the more common professions out there, you need to get used to letting people in on the details. It may not seem like a big deal, but to your clients, they need to understand what they're getting into before they can let yourself into their lives. You can't expect them to trust you if they don't know how it all works.

As you learn more about yourself and gain experience, life coaching will start to take on different meanings. But for the sake of your clients, it's best that you start with a simple, but insightful definition. Life coaching is all about helping people improve their lives.

Your job as a coach is to help people reach their full potential. Whether it's helping them tap into their skills, working with them to find their purpose, or motivating them to reach their goals. Your task is to support them in making their lives better than it before they first started working with you.

A life coach can do many things. I know the concept of coaching may seem very general to you right now, but as you go along the learning process, you'll realize which areas you fit in the most, and eventually, you'll be able to choose a specific area of expertise.

But for starters, here are a few things you can do as a life coach:

- Help clients understand and uphold their set of values

- Listen to their concerns and act as a sounding board for their thoughts and ideas

- Provide emotional and motivational support, especially during crucial decision making opportunities

- Help them identify and get rid of their limiting belief

- Offer guidance that will help them create a clearer vision of their future

- Encourage them to aim high and work towards their set goals

Coaching is different from therapy because it puts different concepts together for the sole purpose of helping your clients live better lives. Coaches work with clients to motivate them to reach certain life goals while therapists work with people to help them with any emotional or behavioral traumas that they may be experiencing. Coaches tend to use their own personal experiences to help clients get a better grasp of their situation, while therapists rarely disclose anything about themselves. Coaches focus more on circumstances and opportunities that will solve a problem, while therapists are more interested to know the whole story behind the problem, how the problem came to be in the first place.

Counselling and coaching are two different things so it's important that you always remember that, as a coach, you're not there to figure out what went wrong in their lives, you're there to help them put their resources to good use.

Although coaching is still relatively new field in the industry, it's become quite popular these past years. People are starting to see how a good coaching program can add value to their lives, not just in their professional goals, but also on their own personal goals. What used to be a program dedicated to corporate development has become a thriving industry, with countless professionals and areas of expertise. And with more and more people turning to coaches for professional help and advice, the coaching industry shows no signs of slowing down any time soon.

As you can see, there are a lot of opportunities for a budding life coach such as yourself. If deep down, you've always wanted to help people change their lives, then life coaching might be the perfect career path for you. As long as there are people who dream of making their lives better, there will always be a need for good life coaches.

CHAPTER 2

The Purpose of Life Coaching

Although the concept life coaching may seem foreign to many people, the main process is designed to help people or teams achieve their full potential. It's used to encourage people to find their purpose and achieve goals faster.

Many people see coaching as a form of counseling, while others look at it as a way to solve problems. There are also those who link coaching to goal setting and achievement. While these are all acceptable purposes of life coaching, it's important that you see it as a beneficial tool that could eventually contribute to your growth. More than just a process, it's actually an investment on yourself that will pay for itself in the long run. Big companies and organizations have seen the long term benefits of investing in lending support and development to their staff and that it's become common for emerging leaders and future managers to undergo some form of coaching in the office. Coaching is all about adding value to your skills, experiences, and life.

I know a lot of you are still discontent with what you have achieved so far. Whether you've just started out your career or you're already approaching retirement years, you probably have personal goals and desires that you still want to achieve. There's nothing wrong with wanting more, in fact, it's inspiring to see people want to go beyond their own expectations. But in order to strive for more, you need to know what kind of goals to set, and how to get there. A coach can help make the journey easier for you.

CHAPTER 3

Areas in Your Life a Life Coach Can Assist

People seek out coaching for many different reasons. Some clients need help dealing with specific concerns like weight loss or career development, while others want to feel more in control over their lives. Whatever their reason may be, at the end of the day, it all boils down to one thing. People want to be happier and live more fulfilling lives.

And because living in this fast paced world is only getting more challenging for some, clients seek out life coaches for support, encouragement, and valuable advice on how to live meaningful lives. It's not enough that you live your life according to how others define success. You need to start living your life with purpose. A life coach can help you become more successful and achieve whatever goals you set for yourself. If you're not happy with your current reality, a life coach will help you craft a whole new one. Here are just a few areas in life where having a life coach can help.

Lose weight

An effective life coach can help you get a grasp of both the emotional, mental, and circumstantial obstacles that prevent you from losing weight. If you've been trying to lose those extra pounds, with very little success, you need a coach who will help you eliminate the obstacles that come between you and your ideal weight. A coach can provide you with some form of structure as you work through those weight loss challenges. Not only will you feel committed to yourself, but you'll also feel committed to your coach.

Stop vices

A good coach understands that vices often stem from addictions, addictions that can take hold of you and all your future decisions if you don't take measures to control it. A coach will help you stand firm on your battle against addiction and offer strategies so that you can break away from the habit for good.

Get organized

A coach can also help you deal with issues that may seem too trivial to be bothered with, like keeping your home and your workspace more organized. If your cluttered home or messy work area is caused by underlying issues that you still haven't come to terms with, then a coach will be able to bring those issues to light.

Become more productive

You probably want to know the secret to becoming more productive and getting things done. Sure you might feel motivated in the beginning, but once the excitement wears off, you'll feel like you're back where you first started. A good coach can equip you with the skills that you need to be able to function better. He or she will look at your working process and help you create new methods to get things done efficiently and effectively.

Learn to recognize and grab on to career breakthroughs

Since most of us are destined to spend almost 1/3 of our lives journeying through career changes, having a coach who will help you recognize and grab on to career breakthroughs can definitely make the whole journey much easier. With the help of tests and structured assignments, a coach can help you figure out a career plan
that will take you to greater heights.

Find long lasting happiness

While happiness may seem like a fluid concept, it's one of the top reasons why people resort to coaching in the first place. All for the pursuit of happiness. If you feel dissatisfied with your life and you're trying to understand what happiness really is, a coach can help you come to terms with your own definition of happiness.

Develop meaningful relationships with people around you

Developing relationships require work and commitment on your end so if you feel distant and isolated because you don't seem to have a good relationship with the people around you, then a coach can help you overcome any issues that are stopping you from reaching out to your family and friends. A coach will give you insight on how you can become more aware of your negative patterns and help you create strategies to overcome them. By changing your behavior, you'll find it easier to foster healthy relationships with family and friends.

Expand your social circle

A coach can also equip you with the skills you need in order to expand your social circle. Forming friendships should be a natural and easy thing to do, but since we live in a more complicated world, it can be somewhat of a challenge, especially for those who aren't naturally outgoing. If you feel like getting out there poses more risks than it's worth, a coach can offer you the support and skills that you need to get yourself out there.

Start and manage a business

Starting and a managing a business can be very overwhelming if you're going to take on the challenge on your own. If you want to move forward, you need someone who will help you keep your eyes on the prize even with the countless tasks you have at hand. A coach can walk you through the challenges, whether big or small, and motivate you to reach your goals, one step at a time.

Define your own personal success and create a gameplan to help you succeed

It doesn't matter which areas of your life you would like to improve, what matters is that you succeed based on your own personal definition of success. With the help and empowerment of a coach, you'll understand what it takes to be a success.

CHAPTER 4

Your Identity and Reason

As a coach, being able to help people find their purpose may seem very exciting, but you can't expect to be an effective coach without first defining your own identity and reason. The first thing that you need to do is determine what exactly you believe in and the things that you stand for. By understanding your identity and reason, you'll be empowered to share what you know to others, your beliefs, values, and even experiences. Here a short step by step guide on how you can get started on developing your own identity and reason, not just as a life coach, but as a human being as well.

Claiming your identity

Identity is what sets you apart from everyone else. It's not just about knowing who you are, but it's knowing what you believe in and the things that you are passionate about. Claiming your identity may seem a bit of a challenge, but once you start to understand your core values and establish your belief system, you'll feel more confident to help others on the paths to self-discovery. You aren't qualified to help others understand their purpose and identity if you don't know what yours is.

Setting your motivation

Once you develop a better understanding of your identity, it will be much easier for you to share what you know and believe in others. And in sharing what you know and believe in, you'll be able to help others find their own identity. This then becomes your main driving force in becoming a life coach. You're not just in it for the knowledge, but you're mainly in it because it will help people live better and more fulfilled lives.

Finding your voice

In order to impact other peoples' lives, you need to find your distinct voice. There are many people who struggle finding their purpose because they lose track of who to listen to. Don't just be another faceless voice in the crowd. If you want to be a catalyst for change in other peoples' lives, you need to be bold and unafraid to express your thoughts and ideas. If you have something worthwhile to share, don't be afraid to express it out loud. Find a medium that will best suit your communication style. Whether it's in writing, through lectures, or even one on one sessions, you need to develop a platform where you can freely express your knowledge and expertise.

Establishing control in your life

In order for your clients to trust you in helping them take control over their lives, you need to foremost be a role model for control. And you gain control by deciding on what your values are, and living out those values. Are you all about developing integrity in the workplace? Or are you in pursuit of knowledge that will further hone your talents and skills? Or are your values set on bringing families together? Once you've established your core values, people who need help in those specific areas will naturally gravitate towards you for advice. Part of establishing control is laying out personal experiences, both good and bad, for everyone to see. Look at your personal experiences not just as reasons for celebration, but also as sources of hope for other people.

Empowering others to make a change

In the end, your main identity and reason as a life coach is to empower others to make choices that will lead to long lasting change. It's easy to feel overwhelmed by the negative circumstances in your life but if you're serious about being a motivator, you need to put your own issues aside and work on becoming a true leader. The most effective way to empower others is to practice what you preach. Speak the truth, keep your intentions transparent, be a person who values integrity. Not only will this help establish your credibility as a life coach, but it also draws people to you. When you make it your purpose to empower others and stop focusing on your own agenda, you naturally become a source of inspiration.

CHAPTER 5

The Qualities of a Great Life Coach

Becoming a life coach isn't just about building a successful practice; it's about being there to touch people's lives and propelling them to greater heights. Unfortunately, there are so called coaches who look at life coaching as an easy paycheck and don't even bother improving themselves. It's these people who give coaching a bad name. So if you're serious about becoming a life coach, and becoming a really good one at that, here are the 10 qualities that you need to develop.

Have a vision

A life coach should always keep the vision in front and in center. Before you start your practice, write down what you would like to achieve, in one sentence, on a piece of paper. Think of it as your personal mission/vision. Make sure it represents who you are as a life coach well. Having a vision for yourself will help keep you on the right track.

Value education

You're not in the business of simply telling people what they should do and not do. You're in the business of helping people find ways to live fulfilling lives. This is why it's important that you value education. You need to always keep an eye out for new strategies and techniques that will not only improve your practice, but also benefit your clients in the long run.

Dedicate time to personal development

You can't be a good life coach without working on your development. A good life coach is someone who pursues education tirelessly and finds ways to develop his or her methods. Since you'll be working with different personalities, you need to constantly educate yourself on how you can relate with your clients. Life coaching is a never ending learning experience. If you think otherwise, then you're probably in the wrong business.

Have a strong sense of dedication and commitment

A coach seldom takes no for an answer. No matter how many setbacks there are, a good coach will find ways to go around those setbacks and continue fighting until situation improves. Having a strong sense of dedication and commitment is important because it will make your clients feel safe and secure. When they see the level of commitment you're putting into their welfare, they'll continue to trust and cooperate with you. And in this line of work, we all know how crucial trust and cooperation is.

Know the importance of preparation

An effective life coach will never go to a consultation or lecture without preparing for it first. Always remember that when clients come to see you, they're not just there for the strategies that you set, but they also expect to find a role model, a credible figure that they can look up to whatever stage of the coaching process you're in, your clients deserve the best you can give. And the only way that you'll be able to do that is through ample preparation.

Develop excellent communication skills

A coach needs to be able to make difficult concepts more relatable to their clients. You need to be able to communicate effectively in order for clients to take notice. And you're not just using words to express information; you also need to know how to use emotion. Before you can translate concepts into action, you need to be able to communicate them well to your clients.

Foster healthy relationships

As a coach, you need to be the initiator to most social interactions. You're the one who will keep everything in balance so it's crucial that you take every means to understand and develop relationships with your clients. You need to understand their needs, wants, and even how they're motivated. It's also important that you make yourself visible every chance you get so that you're seen as easily approachable for any type of situation your clients may bring to the table.

Be a master at decision making

Most people already have their plates full when it comes to decision making so don't be surprised if clients come up to asking what you would do at a certain situation. Clients rely on you to make sound decisions that will help them get to their goals. As a coach, you need to be the one to steer your clients towards the right direction.

Work on being self-aware

Confidence is key in having a successful coaching practice. In order to be able to give your clients the attention and coaching they deserve, you need to have faith in yourself and your leadership capabilities. This is why you need to constantly work on being self-aware. You know how to make the most of your strengths and how to downplay your weaknesses. A coach should know himself, and know himself well.

Be passionate about your craft

A good coach isn't just passionate about life; he or she is also passionate about the craft. This is the root of all your endeavors. If you're passionate about changing peoples' lives, the passion is likely to pass on to your clients, and thus, they'll also become passionate about everything you stand for.

CHAPTER 6

Life Coach Specialization

Once you've developed the right qualities to become an effective coach, the next step is to find your life coach specialization. Even though life coaches can specialize in many different areas, you need to work on having one specialty that will set you apart from the other life coaches out there. You need to have one area that you can focus on if you want to be considered the industry expert.

So how you do you find your specialization? By finding your specific niche. This approach will not only attract the right kind of clients to your practice, but it will also help you stay focused on what you're good at. Why waste time trying to be a 'jack of all trades' when you can offer specialized strategies that will work on your niche? As enticing as it is to want to try to fix everything, you need to accept the reality that you can't address all types of concerns. For example, how are you going to advice parents on how to raise well rounded children, when you don't have children of your own? As a life coach, you're not just drawing out stock knowledge to help people. You also need to have personal experience in the area that you want to specialize in. It's basically capitalizing on what you know.

- Know who you are as a coach and as a person

- Know your passions

- Know your style

- Know your strengths

Here are just a few niches that you might want to consider in choosing your area of expertise:

- Personal development
  > Confidence
  > Leadership
  > Motivation
  > Stress management

- Relationships
  > Social skills
  > Parent coaching

- Business coaching

- Finances

- Health

- Spirituality

Becoming a specialist allows you to offer better service to your clients. You become a qualified professional that people will want to seek out. If you can address specific needs competently, you'll be able to increase your expertise, as well focus on developing what you're particularly effective at. The only way that you'll be able to boost your clientele is by being credible with your chosen niche. It's not the number of strategies that you come up with that will make you a good coach. It's how you work in improving your service for your clients.

CHAPTER 7

Starting Your Life Coach Career

Starting your life coach career doesn't begin with setting up an office, or printing business cards. It starts when you find a client who comes to you for help. Here a step by step guide on how you can start your coaching career, even in the comforts of your own home.

Build rapport with potential clients

After deciding on a specialization, try imagining the type of people who are in need of your specific coaching style. Create a profile of your target client, his wants, needs, fears, and even lifestyle. Once you have a profile up, try to figure out where you're likely to find this client.

Set a free consultation

If you're just starting out, be ready to shell out a lot of free consultations to build your credibility up. You'll be in competition with other life coaches who have started their practices before you so you need to lure in potential clients with a freebie. If you're marketing yourself online for example, why not set up a free trial? This way, you'll be able to get your first taste of coaching someone.

Bring value to the table

Just like in any other business, you should always prioritize bringing value to the table. You need to offer your services in a way that won't turn your potential clients away. Always capitalize on the benefits that you can offer. Bring the problem to light and specify ways that you can help them overcome that. Whether it's losing weight or getting a better job, show your potential clients that with your help, they can act on any problem they may have.

Prepare to overcome objections

You will meet one or two potential clients who will come to you with objections in their head. Objections in business terms are things that bar a sale from happening. Objections come in many forms so the key to squashing them is by detecting they exist early on. If you sense that a person is hesitant to avail your services because of certain reasons, try to find ways to go around that. You need to remove all doubt if you want potential clients to trust you.

Minimize the risks

People will hesitate making changes, especially if they don't feel confident about these changes in the first place. This is why you need to have a strategy in place that will show them how you can minimize risks. Make your offer so compelling and risk free that they won't have any other choice than to accept it. Always make them feel safe and secure because if you come off as untrustworthy, no one will want to come near you, more so accept life coaching from you.

Close the sale

Once you see your potential clients start to warm up to your service, don't forget to close the sale. Ask them to make a decision to commit with you in the most harmless way you can.

Conclusion

Thank you again for purchasing this book!

I hope this book was able to help you understand the basics on how to become a life coach. I know starting your own practice may seem a bit daunting right now, but once you get through the basics, the next step is to get out there and make your mark in the world.

I hope this book has given you motivation to become the best life coach you can possibly be. No matter where you find yourself in the world, always remember that at the end of the day, it's not just your skills or strategies that will set you apart from the other coaches; it's your genuine concern for their welfare and development.

Finally, if you enjoyed this book, then I'd like to ask you for a favor, would you be kind enough to leave a review for this book on Amazon? It'd be greatly appreciated!

CPSIA information can be obtained
at www.ICGtesting.com
Printed in the USA
BVHW030710081218
535101BV00002B/209/P